HAPPY BIRTHDAY

CU00997027

CONTENTS   Page

ACKNOWLEDGEMENTS

Happy Birthday Anyway! is based on *Ageing*, a report from the Board for Social Responsibility (Church House Publishing, 1990). The working party which produced the report was set up by the Board's Social Policy Committee and was chaired by Mr Raymond Clarke. The full report costs £5.95, and is available from bookshops and from Church House Bookshop, 31 Great Smith Street, London SW1P 3BN. Further copies of the study guide are available from bookshops, Church House Bookshop, or from BSR, Church House, Great Smith Street, London SW1P 3NZ.

The Board is very grateful to Joan King, Family Work Co-ordinator at Scripture Union, for her help in preparing this guide. The Church House staff involved were Alison Webster, Deborah Cunningham and Christina Forde.

This study guide has only the authority of the Board by which it was prepared.

Published 1990 for the General Synod Board for Social Responsibility by Church House Publishing.

ISBN 0 7151 6575 5

GS 941

Cover design *by Iain Colquhoun*

Cartoons *by Neil Pinchbeck*

Printed in England by The Campfield Press, St. Albans.

Introduction

'Roses are red, violets are blue. It's alright to be fifty...if you feel twenty two!'

The jokes in birthday cards show that we are often uncertain about getting older. Is it something to celebrate or to regret?

ROSES ARE RED____

Ageing is the process of growing old, not just old age. Two people may be seventy years old, but one may be a young seventy while the other is old. Our life experiences, personalities and health all influence how we age. That is why old age needs to be considered with the whole life-span in mind.

It is a good time to be interested in ageing. More people are living longer. Often they live alone. Changes in health and welfare services are upon us. Family patterns are changing. In addition, elderly people may feel written off once they no longer have the status of a job. But most retiring sixty- or sixty-five-year-old people can in fact look forward to many years of activity in which to grow, learn, and make their contribution to home, church and community life.

Although few people go to Church regularly, many turn to it at important times in their lives, such as the birth of a child, getting married, or when someone they love dies. Ageing is about moving through these life events and the Church is often involved.

All these things are opportunities for the mission and ministry of the Church.

1

Using This Guide

This guide is based on *Ageing*, a report from the Board for Social Responsibility. It gives information about ageing in Britain and emphasises a number of challenges for churches and for policy-makers.

After giving the main findings of the Report, the guide is divided into sections on different themes. Each section provides information, ideas for things to do and questions to explore, as well as direct points from the Report.

The guide can be used by individuals or, even better, by groups. It will help you think about ageing - both how it affects you personally, and what we might need to do as a society. There are some issues best explored with others because they need a group response. So we suggest that churches consider using all or some of the sections with, for example, housegroups, pastoral care groups, worship groups, church councils. It could also be a starting point for a meeting with local people from voluntary organisations, or from the health and welfare services.

When using each section, it is probably best to consider the information first and then go on to explore the questions and suggested activities listed under the heading 'Action'. The questions are there to help you reflect on issues of ageing and to work out practical steps which may be taken by you and your church.

The Report aims to:

- present the facts about ageing in British society;
- reflect on how people age and what they feel about growing older;
- look at the kinds of social policies which are needed;
- discover how Christians respond;
- consider what the Church is doing in this field, and suggest what more could be done.

What The Report Says

- It says that people are unique and have a contribution to make whatever their age.

- *It emphasises change and growth throughout life while attempting to be honest about loss and pain in the experience of ageing.*

- It looks at what the Bible has to say about ageing.

- *It questions the negative attitudes to ageing which are common in society. It says that these come from the fear of physical and mental decline and dying, and from believing that we are only successful if we are productive.*

- It reminds us of the maturity of judgement that can come with growing older, and with having space and time to think and dream dreams. Ageing is something to celebrate.

- *It describes the welfare services which are there to support people in their old age.*

- It says that much imaginative work is done by the medical profession, social services and residential staff working with elderly people but it expresses concern that the quality and availability of services for elderly people vary across the country.

- *It recognises that in the future voluntary and private agencies will play a bigger part in running welfare services.*

- *It calls for the continued funding of basic welfare services across the country through taxation.*

- It asks policy makers and planners to be aware of gender issues - there are more elderly women than men and more women caring for frail and dependent relatives.

- *It argues that it is now time, in this country and abroad, to give special attention to the needs of elderly people.*

- It says that education does not stop when you leave school. Older people can gain much from adult education and more adult education opportunities are needed.

- *It encourages the churches to develop a more positive approach to their work with elderly people in the Church and wider community, and to give more support to carers.*

- It challenges churches to examine their responsibility for elderly clergy and lay workers.

- *It argues that the Church must look closely at public policies which affect people's lives, and be ready to speak out when necessary.*

I The Facts Of The Matter

There are more elderly people in society than ever before, and proportionately fewer younger people.

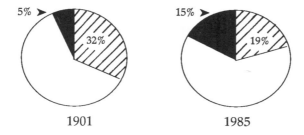

| 1901 | 1985 |

■ Elderly people (population over 65 years in UK)
▨ Children (population under 15 in UK)
Based on Social Trends 17 and 20. HMSO.

Life expectancy has increased dramatically this century. This table shows how long a baby born in 1906 and 1985 could expect to live.

	Male	Female
1906	48	~~49~~ 52
1985	70	77

Based on Population Trends 19. HMSO.

- There are now over 10 million people of pensionable age in the UK.

- The number of people reaching their 100th birthday increased nearly ten times between 1951 and 1981.

Where elderly people live

- Over 50% of elderly people own their own home.

- Less than 5% of elderly people live in residential care.

- Over 95% live in the community.

- The number of over-65s living alone is rising; 36% lived alone in 1985.

THERE ARE TWICE AS MANY WOMEN OVER 65 AS MEN

85   65   45   25   5

SEVERAL GENERATIONS OF ONE FAMILY MAY HAVE FINISHED BRINGING UP THEIR OWN CHILDREN. PEOPLE OVER 60 MAY BE CARING FOR THEIR OWN PARENTS OR ELDERLY RELATIVES.

- The proportion of elderly people in the population varies from area to area. In 1985, East Sussex had the highest proportion of retired people in the country.

- A growing percentage of elderly people in the future will be from minority ethnic groups. Their special needs will have to be addressed.

❏ State pensions and benefits form a very important part of the incomes of the majority of older people.

❏ There are fewer young people to join the workforce, generate the wealth and pay the taxes which provide the resources for pensions and services provided by the state.

❏ After finishing work and raising a family, most people still have 10, 20, 30 years or more life ahead of them.

Action

Consider: What do these facts mean for
a) the society in which people age?
b) the ministry and witness of the Church?

The Report asks the Church and policy-makers to take seriously the changes in the age structure of society. It suggests that these changes will affect the context in which people live and age in the next 20 years.

2. Problems And Possibilities

Attitudes to ageing

☐ Old people feel, and often are, undervalued in society because we rate work, productivity and wealth creation so highly.

☐ Negative attitudes to older people are common. There are many stereotypes which make elderly people seem figures of fun, pathetic, domineering or unbalanced. Consider Dot, Lou and Ethel in *EastEnders* or Compo in *Last of the Summer Wine*.

☐ Discrimination or prejudice against people on the basis of their age is called ageism. It is sometimes heard in the way we talk.
'Look at that old biddy!'
'You're talking like an old woman!'
'He's too old to understand computers!'

HE'S TOO OLD TO UNDERSTAND COMPUTERS?!

☐ Negative images affect the way old people are treated in society. They also influence how old people see themselves.

- Ageing is associated with loss of work, health, activity and energy.

- There are painful experiences which need to be faced as we grow old *but* there is much that is hopeful of which we hear little.

- Young people are also sometimes discriminated against on grounds of age.

VIC, SO DISTINGUISHED – BUT ELIZABETH ....

- Ageism tends to flatter men but threaten women.
  'Vic looks so distinguished now that his hair is grey.'
  'Elizabeth's looking old. She needs some Grecian 2000.'

Action

1. Think about what it means to you to grow older. What is good about it?

2. Think of someone who was old when you were a child. What was special about them? How did you feel about them? What did you learn from them? If you are in a group share your thinking.

3. Discover some of the gains and losses in growing older. When you have the opportunity, perhaps in a housegroup, ask the over-60s to share one thing:

   ❑ they have learned since they were 60;
   ❑ they enjoy about being older;
   ❑ they find difficult about being older;
   ❑ they like to remember from the past.

4. Use encouraging examples of ageing in the teaching and learning activities of the Church, e.g. in sermons, housegroups, children's groups and clubs.

The Report calls on the Church to find ways of helping people to view ageing positively and argues:

'Cultures which place high value on economic activity and individual productivity and consumption tend to have great difficulty in viewing the ageing process positively.' (Ageing, p.140)

Dependence and independence

Is independence a virtue? Is dependence a bad thing? One might think so in our society.

Such beliefs need challenging by Christians. People move through stages of dependence and independence. Babies are dependent but becoming more independent. There are times in all of our lives when we are especially vulnerable and weak. Towards the end of life some people will require the constant physical care that they needed as young children. These people can be a means of grace.

A helpful way to think of life is in stages. It is sometimes said that there is a *First Age* of childhood and schooling, a *Second Age* of work and raising a family, a *Third Age* of active independence and a *Fourth Age* of dependence and dignity.

Action

Consider the passage in Luke 2.22-38.

Here we have two people, Simeon and Anna, reaching the end of life. Try to put yourself in their shoes. Think about what is happening in the story.

In what ways does this passage give value to old and 'unproductive' people?

The Report questions

❏ the bad press which ageing gets;
❏ the idea that elderly black people have no need for special services because of strong family and community support;
❏ the view that elderly people should be protected at all costs from taking risks.

11

Let's be positive

What's good about getting older?

Perhaps there is more time to:

- [ ] make sense of the past and plan the future.
- [ ] grow and be renewed.
- [ ] face important questions: who am I? what's happening to me?
- [ ] care for our own health.
- [ ] take up new interests and continue to learn.
- [ ] enjoy close relationships and keep friendships going.
- [ ] make changes.
- [ ] take up voluntary activity.
- [ ] develop relationships with grown-up children, grandchildren and great-grandchildren.

TIME TO DEVELOP RELATIONSHIPS WITH GRANDCHILDREN..

Jack was 67. After two years adjusting to being at home, thinking about his own life and facing the questions that come with retirement, he reassessed his values and decided to take a step of faith. He was confirmed. Now, almost ten years later, he is still active in the local church and community. He has found his particular role in supporting elderly single people and people who have been bereaved.

Action

1. Think about the new opportunities you may have as you continue to age.

2. Encourage the elderly people you know to see that there are many activities they can be involved in.

The Report emphasises that getting older does not necessarily mean you enjoy life less. It says that ageing can be something to celebrate, not regret.

3. Christian Resources

The Report suggests four ways our Christian faith can help.

1. **The worshipping community** binds together people of all ages who are related through faith in Christ. Together we are enabled to focus on the vision of God who is in and beyond us. Our worship, especially eucharistic worship, helps us to recognise that whatever our difficulties or apparent failures we are forgiven by God.

2. **The Old Testament** encourages us to accept the wisdom and leadership ability that should accompany old age. It recognises that this does not always happen but assures us that God will put things right in God's own time. The dominant mood is one of hope.

3. **The New Testament** calls people to maturity in Christ. It shows that our lives are set in a framework of hope and of eternal life.

4. **Jesus** suffered the ultimate loss - loss of God's presence - while on the cross. His life was complete. He was ready 'to let go', to give up control and to trust God and others to continue his work.

Action

1. In our society models, athletes, beauty queens, young couples in love are seen as shining examples of humanity. Suppose the models of perfect humanity were skilled craftspeople or artists, the wise and patient person overcoming difficulty or the couple whose marriage has flourished over 50 years. How would the world be different? How would older people be viewed in society then? How would that be different from how they are often seen now?

"...THOUGH OUTWARDLY WE ARE WASTING AWAY, YET INWARDLY
WE ARE BEING RENEWED DAY BY DAY" (2 COR 4:16).

2. Psalm 71 is the prayer of an old man. There is a serenity about
it which is characteristic of a long life spent in reliance on God.

Read the psalm and think about the writer's long life.

Past   As he reflects on his life (verses 1-18), how does he see
that he has experienced God?

Present   What is the situation in which the writer finds himself
now and what is his prayer (verse 9-12)?

Future   What are this man's hopes as he lives his life in God's
presence? What does he look forward to (verses 18 and 19)?
What is he going to do in his old age (especially verses
22 and 23)?

Me   Think about your own life. In what ways have you known
God's care and protection? How do you identify with the
writer of Psalm 71?

As you look forward towards old age what are your hopes and fears, recognising that God cares and is with you now and in the future?

Us   If you are in a group share your thoughts about Psalm 71 together.

3. Read 2 Corinthians 4 and 5. Paul is ageing but his inner life is being renewed daily.

❑   In what ways is God at work in him creatively?

❑   What are the losses in physical strength that Paul experiences?

❑   Note how a sense of death and resurrection are both there in his life.

❑   How have you experienced these things in your own life?

The Report calls on the Church

To recognise that everyone is strong and weak at different times in life. We need to bear one another's burdens.

To look at the values behind the current thinking about ageing in the work of policy-makers and those involved in the human sciences.

To consider issues of justice, especially as they affect disadvantaged members of society in their older age.

4. Faith And Ageing

Findings in the report are:

Many old people want to talk about what they have discovered about God during their life.

Many want to explore questions of faith.

Some want spiritual direction.

Most experience losses and bereavement and want to make sense of what has happened. They may need help in facing their own dying and death.

Elderly Christians want to feel included in the worship and witness of their churches, and often have much to give.

Action

1. *One church has a high proportion of elderly people. The church has learned that without their time, experience and insight it would be impoverished.*

   It has realised the importance of worship in the homes of people who are housebound. It has developed a Fellowship of Prayer which enables them to contribute to the life and ministry of the Church.

   How does your church make the most of what elderly people have to give? Does it even know what they have to give? If not, explore ways of finding out.

   How does your church nurture its elderly people in the faith? Is there any action that needs to be taken? For example, recording services for housebound people, midweek Eucharists in people's homes, or keeping them informed of prayer needs.

2. Explore ways of bringing the Gospel to elderly people, especially in this Decade of Evangelism.

3. Look at how your church cares for people who have been bereaved.

4. Would some training on understanding loss and bereavement be helpful for members of your congregation? If so, explore the training materials, resources and courses available in your diocese or through other agencies. The church or diocese may be able to put on a course.

5. Many older people gain a lot through reminiscence - a way of thinking about their lives and learning more about themselves. Where and who are the listeners in your church?

6. Don't forget to use your diocesan specialists.

   For example:

> Family Life Worker
> Adult Education or Training Officer
> Missioner
> Social Responsibility Officer
> Social Worker

The Report recognises that the old images of heaven, earth and hell have gone for most people. Life here and now is widely believed to be the whole story. It urges the Church to think more deeply and talk more openly about dying and death and life beyond.

5. An All-age Community

'Every local church has the potential to be a community of different generations.' (Ageing, p.117)

DIFFERENT GENERATIONS – A WORSHIPPING COMMUNITY...

A few years ago one congregation, made up of people from different generations and ethnic backgrounds, decided to try to build the generations into a worshipping community of God's people. With much prayer, and knowing that change involves risk and pain, the pattern of worship on Sunday mornings was adjusted.

The family Eucharist now begins with age-related learning groups for children and young people while the adults follow the communion service. Sometimes they have a series of sermons and at other times choose special groups. At the peace the children join the adults. The peace lasts for at least half an hour. Coffee and fruit juice is served in the church. People mix, talk, share and play all together across the generations. This is part of their worship. They then continue together with the rest of the communion service.

In a very practical way this 'peace' is helping people at all stages of life understand, love and respect each other. Relationships are being built which it is hoped will strengthen the church to handle the differences that occur between people of different ages.

Action

1. The pattern of worship developed here works well in that particular church. Yours will be different. Consider the age structure of your congregation. Roughly how many people are there in each stage of life?

    First Age   (childhood and schooling)......................

    Second Age (work and raising a family)...............

    Third Age   (active independence)...........................

    Fourth Age   (dependence and dignity).................

2. How are people from these age bands in your church being brought together? Are there any existing activities which may be adapted to enable people from different church groups to relate with each other?

3. Consider the worship services. Do some people feel excluded? If so, what can be done to help them feel more welcome and accepted?

4. Is there any action that needs to be taken to help elderly people feel physically comfortable in church services, e.g. loop systems, lighting, size of print, lavatories which are easy to reach?

5. Is yours a church with a mainly elderly congregation? If so, you will be facing the issues and questions of this life stage together. What are the particular issues people may need help with?

The Report emphasises the value of older people to the whole life of the Church. It encourages churches to find ways of building an all-age community of faith and recognises that some churches are themselves elderly communities. They need to address together the issues faced by all people at that stage of life.

6.   Who Cares? Who Should Care?

Some facts

- Most people have good health well into their 70s.
- There are about 6 million people in Britain, caring for sick, disabled or elderly people.
- Nearly two-thirds of carers are women.
- 80% of carers are looking after relatives.
- Voluntary carers save the state an estimated £24 billion a year in public expenditure.
- Support services for carers are patchy over the country.
- Carers are given little help in understanding the complex state provision and benefits.
- 20% of people over 80 are handicapped by dementia, though not all to the same degree.

CARERS ARE GIVEN LITTLE HELP IN UNDERSTANDING THE COMPLEX STATE PROVISION AND BENEFITS _ _ _ _

A Story

Mary is 76 years old and living alone for the first time in her life. Her husband Tom is in hospital permanently and sometimes does not recognise her when she visits him. The hospital car service costs her £5 each time she travels to the hospital. There is no direct public transport from where she lives. Neighbours try to give her lifts at weekends.

Mary is lonely. Her daughter, a grandparent herself, lives in New Zealand, while her son also lives many miles away. It is hard to make decisions alone. The house feels too big but she cannot face moving. At times she is bewildered by her feelings. She is angry with Tom for leaving her with his tool shed to sort out. She feels guilty about being angry. 'Poor Tom. I know it's not his fault. I'm glad he is well cared for,' she says. Then fear sets in. Aware of the aches and pains that come with age, Mary wonders who will care for her.

When Tom became ill she cared for him for six long years. They slowly drifted away from the church. Apart from one friend and an occasional church pastoral care visitor, few people came to the home. Only in the last year that Tom was at home did she receive practical help from the community nurse and home help. The only break came during Tom's weekly visit to the day centre, when she had a game of cards with friends and visited the shops. Otherwise the main person in her life was Tom. Now he is not there, yet he is still alive.

Action

1. If Mary and Tom were living in your parish how would you know about them? How would your church support them?

2. In what ways does the Church express its love to people who are ill for a long time and to those who look after them?

3. What could be done to create more effective support for the absent members of the Church, and for those in the wider community suffering from long-term stress because they are carers?

4. Find out what support there is for carers in your area and the contribution Christians might make to this. Make sure that the voluntary carers in your church can get this information.

5. Keep abreast of public policy and the role of the state in welfare provision. Be ready to speak out where necessary.

6. Discover who the professional carers are in your church and community. These are the people who support voluntary carers. Encourage them in what they do and pray for them.

The Report suggests that dioceses should consider setting up special interest groups on ageing to find out what is going on locally, and what might be needed. This is already happening in some places. It also suggests that the training needs of lay people and clergy should be addressed.

The Report says that caring for a dependent person can be very rewarding; it can also be lonely and tiring.

The Report calls on the Church to offer a practical response to those suffering from dementia and to find ways of helping them to feel loved by God and by Christians. This will mean learning to communicate in different ways, both pastorally and in worship. It will mean learning to use the senses (sight, sound, touch, smell and taste) in worship.

> 'If prejudice is to be overcome and people with dementia are to be given adequate spiritual sustenance they must be found a place within the Body of Christ. Then when individual memory is lost the Body of Christ can remember together for them... declare the faith together for them... uphold that person and those who love them in the hope of the resurrection.' (Ageing, p.94)

7.   Policies For Our Country

Background

As people grow older and come to the end of their lives, they may need support of different kinds - good medical care, more help, safe housing. Knowing that help is available does a lot to give elderly people peace of mind.

For the last forty years, many of our welfare services have been provided out of general taxation. Recently this welfare state has been questioned for two main reasons:

◻   increasing costs, which can mean that care has to be rationed.

◻   changing opinions about how much the state should be involved in providing support.

What is happening now?

Current Government policy aims to increase private and voluntary welfare provision.

Community care services - support for elderly people, people with mental handicaps, with disabilities and with mental illness living at home - are being reorganised.

The *number* of places for elderly people in private residential care has grown enormously in the last 10 years. However the *proportion* of elderly people in residential care today is about the same as in 1900.

Surveys have shown that standards of care in residential homes vary. Residents do not always have the privacy and dignity they need.

The benefits system has also been changed recently. Some benefits which were granted of right have now become discretionary under the Social Fund. Many older people are now better off, but an Age Concern survey (1989) shows that some older people would rather suffer hardship than ask for a loan.

Despite attempts to make improvements, many people live out their old age in poor housing, on very low incomes, and with little professional support.

In the next 20 years, more people from minority ethnic groups will reach old age. The needs of elderly black people have often been neglected, but they are beginning to receive more attention.

Action

1. Find out about Government policy on welfare benefits and its effects on elderly people.

2. Consider ways in which the local church might be more involved in community projects.

3. Find out where elderly people can get advice and practical help. Have the information available for them.

4. Be practical!

The Report argues that the state should keep the major responsibility for provision of services and that it should monitor the work done by all agencies. The private and voluntary sectors are very important but are unlikely to be able to provide basic services of good quality across the country.

8. Finally......

Now that you have used this booklet you may like to think about the following:

As I get older, I feel good about...

As I get older, I need to be aware of.....

As I get older, I look forward to.....

In its work with people of all ages

Our church is good at...

Our church needs help with....

Our church is going to.....

Let's end with the strong and hopeful words of Psalm 121:

If I lift up my eyes to the hills, where shall I find help?
My help comes only from the Lord, maker of heaven and earth.
He will not let your foot stumble; he who guards you will not sleep.
The guardian of Israel never slumbers, never sleeps.
The Lord is your guardian, your protector at your right hand.
The sun will not strike you by day nor the moon by night.
The Lord will guard you against all harm; he will guard your life.
The Lord will guard you as you come and go, now and for
evermore.   (Revised English Bible).

BOOKS AND RESOURCES

Growing Older. Una Kroll. Fount, 1988.

At Home in a Home. Pat Young. Age Concern, 1988.

Loneliness - How to Overcome It. Val Marriott and Terry Timblick. Age Concern, 1988.

Carers: Out of Sight, Out of Mind. A Jubilee Centre Video, 1990. (3 Hooper Street, Cambridge, CB1 2NZ)

Living, Loving and Ageing: Sexual and Personal Relationships in later life. Wendy Greengross and Sally Greengross. Age Concern, 1989.

From Generation to Generation. Julia Burton-Jones. Jubilee Centre (Cambridge) Research Paper No 9. 1990. There is also a Jubilee Centre video on carers.

Leaves on the Tree. National Society and Church House Publishing, 1990.

It's My Duty Isn't It? Jill Pitkeathley. Souvenir, 1989.

Life Later On: Older People in the Church. Ann Webber. Triangle/SPCK 1990.

Distance Learning Materials on Ageing. The Training Unit, Scripture Union National Training Centre, 26-30 Heathcoat Street, Nottingham NG1 3AA. These materials are for individual or group use to help you understand various aspects of the ageing process, and how to support those who care for old people. Available early 1991.

Bringing the Church Family Together. Distance learning materials for use in groups to help people learn skills for planning and leading all-age worship and learning activities. The pack also contains ideas and programme suggestions for use in churches. Available January 1991 from Scripture Union. (Address above).

ORGANISATIONS

Age Concern England
Astral House
1268 London Road
London SW16 4ER
Tel: 081-679 8000

Age Concern provides training, information and research for retired people and those who work with them.

Age Concern Institute of Gerontology
King's College London
Cornwall House Annexe
Waterloo Road
London SE1 8TX
Tel: 071-872 3035

The Institute is involved in research and teaching on all aspects of ageing.

Alzheimer's Disease Society
158-160 Balham High Road
London SW12 9BN
Tel: 081-675 6557

Publishes a newsletter, factsheets and a guide for people caring for people caring for someone with dementia. A network of local branches supports those suffering from dementia and their families.

Carers' National Association
29 Chilworth Mews
London W2 3RG
Tel: 071-724 7776

Offers an information and advice service for carers and brings carers' needs and problems to the attention of government and media.

Centre for Policy on Ageing
25-31 Ironmonger Row
London EC1V 3QP
Tel: 071-253 1787

Investigates areas of concern affecting older people and urges people responsible to take appropriate action.

Christian Council on Ageing
The Old Court
Greens Norton
Nr Towcester
Northants NN12 8BS
Tel: 0327 50481

CCOA's aim is to integrate older people into the life of local churches and communities and to improve their pastoral care. Counselling and pre-retirement courses are run.

Cruse - Bereavement Care
Cruse House
126 Sheen Road
Richmond
Surrey TW9 1UR
Tel: 081-940 4818

Cruse publishes a range of literature and offers counselling, advice and social opportunities for bereaved people.

Help the Aged
16-18 St James's Walk
London EC1R 0BE
Tel: 071-253 0253

A national charity which aims to improve the quality of life of elderly people in the UK and overseas.

National Association of Citizens Advice Bureaux
115-123 Pentonville Road
London N1 9LZ
Tel: 071-833 2181

Provides information and advice on social security benefits, housing, family, personal matters, money and consumer complaints.

Pre-Retirement Association of Great Britain and Northern Ireland
19 Undine Street
Tooting
London SW17 8PP
Tel: 081-767 3225

Advises on pre-retirement education and keeps in contact with local groups throughout the UK.

Relate
Herbert Gray College
Little Church Street
Rugby CV21 3AP
Tel: 0788 73241

Relate sees many couples over 60 who find discussing their problems with a counsellor helpful. It is best to contact your local branch. The number will be in the telephone book.